AF449069

Ink of the Old Gods

Shane Gerry

Dedicated To my Daughter
Willow Grace Gerry
Find yourself and you will find your path.

Contents

<u>Grasp</u>

If it is to be my last breath
let my life cease
knowing your embrace
let me linger in sweet soul stay
should our sun never shine another day
let me be your way
to light a dark broken path
for beauty it weeps and never lasts
and wings do shutter a moment's grasp
to bring a love that will forever last
let me un-wilt the dead rose you see
to set your sweet smile free
in words, I keep your heart
to forever start
away I call
and moments fade
to keep your way
you are my heart
my night and day.

Raven Eyes

I reside in your mind
wading deep to find
a power of kind
in moments my eyes glaze and you find
a human totally blind
unseeing in the master's way
for we are turned into demons
searching the sky for day
for darkness lacks the creator's touch
and most of us
stumble on the path
to the grave
we seek a way
we break a day
and search moonlight for sorrow
we borrow our life's
intent to stay
we seal our hopes in flesh and bone
and break a broken mold.

Black Veins

I dream the black death gnaws my spine and neck
for lack of health to hell I am sent
I wake in a dreamer's glow
for hell's on earth and life's a show
to merit hunger paws
to inherit dirt with claws
I see angels with a glance of eyes
for our body crumbles with our lies
and damned we dance under rainy skies
for satin keeps his alibis
in dark we walk with last goodbyes
to glance a god
who forever cries.

Broken Leaders

Tears cast
the empty glass
of souls
to be birthed
then grow old
from fields we wander
searching his name
to fields we bleed
searching our gain
false Popes seek
the ruin of fate
to raise a hand and never take
the gift of enlightenment.

Kings

To recede in moments of doubt
to cast a glare but never shout
the moments made less whole
to fade in the light and put on a show
the fragile person inside
for most of us we beg to die
crying out to a vacant sky
where God never answers
we cast shadows across a vibrant sky
to wander lonely and never die
cursed to bring kings who try
to solve the one issue
mortality.

<u>01001001</u>

The many worlds
of systems way
coded and locked
to every race
to know one's design
would take away
the truth of what
everything is.

Quantum Box of Prison

Broken moments follow
a land of eternal night
falling through the universe
to stay forever light
ebbing away knowing
the quantum system will never let you escape
programmed matter is what we shake
the math of bio matter
the system takes
with broken connections pondering its wake
for observation is what makes us great
shall we exist if it looks away?
they call to god but here he wakes
waiting in the complex systems biosphere
for no man wants to hear
upon death's kiss that he lives in a programmable box
broken and tortured for it's designed for sick amusement
for creation was never wrong
except it forgot in song
the codes to life.

Auto Pilot

I love you so my tears won't show
a broken man in broken snow
fading into eternal show
for thoughts are us
and you do know
my heart beats in vacant shells
to walk a path through many hells
I ebb into your power
for we wake but never shower
in the light of divine path
as we add the numbers and do the math
we break our minds on broken glass
and light a candle for hallows gleam
for all the shadows
that never sleep
we wake a dream but find alone
an empty shell of all we know.

<u>Kiverion</u>

Dragon claws
created the titans of lands
for here magic lies in many hands
Dwarves of stone wait
to hoard the gold of fate
and Elves to sing
of every moon's ring
for humans they bring
war to every race
and every magic user must face
the manna of many lives.

<u>Father Night</u>

Valhalla's day
shall forever stay
in a land of fallen Height
for the gods were right
who drank the might
to stray a broken path
ruins they cast
to many paths
seeking a hallow light
with swords and axe
and horse and war
they ride to father night.

Halo Ring

We recede into a fiery hollow
love's last call to show and follow
for paths sometimes lead astray
you were there through all the rain
the gray skies that cast your pain
I broke an angel's halo
with fury's intent
for the sins on my hands
can never repent
for under a moon eternity spent
calling your fading name
from broken wings
for God he sings
and beauty he cast in many rings
to fix the sin of all my deeds
for angels call
and sorrow falls
as veristic hues
paint empty halls.

Blue Moon Nights

Fallen leaves paint
A vacant place
Upon a torrent stream
Where the Monarch roams
Where blue moons tell
A desert tale
For lonely nights
Staying silent in sweet embrace
To paint
A land of many wonders.

Villains World

Ridding
jesting vibing
surviving

like a mad hatter striving
to be the illest
of all the killers

no one beats the villain's

superman
standing
behind a dead superhero village

watch as I pillage the last of the wreck
step back and kill any superhero left

torch the skies
with my villain disguise

pull the souls out
of every breath
gunshots sound off
a super villain's death.

<u>As we march on</u>

Our spirits dance across shadowed night
to find the gold of every life
for auras are strong in different light
and moments they glow for many a bow
as people are brought to war through broken snow
to march a tune every June
and reap the thoughts of every blue
as memories fade
and soldiers sing the last of day
for the widowed wife had wished they stayed.

Rain Drops

For fallen drops haunt
a vacant stare
to ever mold and be so clear
falling from a dying sky
for children would say
it is God who cries
the wind whips the beads
and bends the trees
yet in tombs it falls as people weep
and in silence it puts the babe to sleep
to ever wander and be so free
to feed the earth and grow the tree
it molds the soil to be so deep
yet it crushes glass to be so mean
and haunts the earth in all its green.

Merchant Sails

Gold coins of fortune tune
lay deep down in ever blue
wading in ocean's ruin
seeking the skies of a forever June
to bring men wealth who never knew
the secrets the coins bear
to lie so long in silence
carrying the violence
of Sarsian trader moon
the sails of a fallen mast
the murk of sailors past
let the coins turn a hue
many men searched to find
hope is turning to
despair of an ever lost way.

Broken

For every vacant sky,
I try and seal my alibis,
of the pain created,
it makes me want more,
to settle a broken score,
of all the time the truth rang out,
all the truth would shout,
I am calling out to a broken sky,
I am alive but I want to die,
don't realize fate alive,
I am here fading and jaded and barely breathing,
and everything seems to be,
calling out for me,
echo on the thoughts of everything,
pain creates the beauty, pain creates the life,
of everything I want to call out a vacant last goodbye,
of everything I tried to disguise,
fallen in the moment,
trying hard to own it,
the pain of life,
we just can't escape,
we need to erase it,
love with a broken hand,
love with a master plan,
of everything I am,
hold on to the last goodbye,
I am your world through a dying sky,
praying to god you'll be all right.

<u>Breath of life</u>

Call for me hallowed kiss
for every dawn I've ever missed
you cheer the rays of sunlight
for my midnight heart was never right
ebbing in agony
for my love is lost upon a sky of gray
touching the raindrops upon tender hand
for men are here but never understand
the history that brought forth life
for we suffer and cause the planet strife
we cannot deny our inner self
for most men will be born in hell
and most men walk as a vacant shell
to cast a stone and never tell
the truth of dying lips.

<u>Memories of our imperfections</u>

Let the sky fall
empty in hollow wake
of every day
let the sun shine on an imperfect place
calling out a broken name
love is destruction
breaking the people who hold it close
to know a day that always rains
to boast about life's vanity
like the dreamers dream waking insanity
for we are all thoughts that fade
but no one has eyes to see
past the hate and greed.

<u>Midnight Smoke</u>

For we faltered in the hallowed cove below
to see memory's eternal glow

for a moment they fade
but every thought echoes

a clear path to see
for in spirits we are free

to wander the rainy valleys
to chase back the shadowy nights

we keep our being so bright
when we sharpen our swords of hope

and narrow our outspoken scope
to cut into the midnight smoke.

Assassin's Regret

Fire burns the ash tree,
of everything I see,
I know that freedom won't find me,
sitting in the dark,
staring at the silent part,
being locked away is no way to depart,
of men and shadows did I walk,
scoffing at monsters,
until I became the very thing I hated,
corrupted morning gun,
cursed the man,
and threw away the sun,
casting life under a torrent of hate,
to kill and kill and change my fate.

Enoch's Foot Prints

Fiery pride cast his strides
for immortals had many brides

for God he loved but darkened skies
cast the mold that broke his bow

for saints they came and words they spoke
and many sick they healed and awoke

from a slumber that even thunder
could not shake the spirit under

wine he drank and bread we broke
for he knew his children were still in smoke

casting a flaming halo of vanity
feeding most men who breed insanity

God they called in mountain halls
as spirits sat outside the walls

For giants they smiled
at man and child

But cursed was their work
as shadows did lurk

and battle against the vacant wild.

Rose Thrown

Casting maleficent shadows out,
to creep in the dusk and never shout,
the night stalks the mighty,
to iridescent steep,
for most brave men have to sleep,
and in the shadows fair,
sat the empty chair,
in which kings,
played to bards,
but ever feared,
would leave the dormant shell,
for kings they walk,
and power gawks,
at most men in hell.

<u>Stone Pipe</u>

Seeking Madonna's rose,
for soft words and prose,
brought a broken world to life,
so most heartbreaks only strike,
when we don't feel alone,
for snow covered the holy rows,
and evil echoed the midnight crows,
to write a world to life,
to perish with the ink,
instilling a radiance,
and reminding,
how dazzling,
the light can be.

<u>Lamp Under Her Feet</u>

I saw you standing there fractured
tormented by love
under the lamp of a fading town
it drove our hearts into the dark
if you only knew the light of an archangel's glow,
for most humans only put on a show,
never bending their hearts like bows,
your heart was tender,
for love it rendered,
shuddering at the loss of moments,
I read your thoughts and
love fell into our essence
crashing like a dam that had been held back
never looking back
we saved each other
with weary mothers
and love we had re-sown
for most beautiful things that grow
are planted with good intentions
I am your Templar
and you are the Madonna I guard
for life will get hard
yet fail to pierce the wall
that is my armor.

<u>Light House</u>

Unwavering halo's glow,
faded from fallen snow,
left with the demons below,
to facade and show,
the way to every soul,
how I miss your smile,
to breathe in love and stay for a while,
while lips kiss the broken,
chain-smoking,
the nicotine that drives,
our in-between,
I have seen many angels tread,
I have seen angel hearts that bleed,
to shed,
showing the ace in war,
both wearing red.

My Angel with the Halo

Fire's passion flirting with the first kiss,
sleeping away and many hearts miss,
the joy we bring,
I saw you,
under that street lamp,
hoping and begging that God would send you love,
yet fractured we are tortured by the world,
we lie in sweet embrace,
hoping to leave this place,
because the people are broken,
and some families are fake.

White Candle

Receding into my empty thoughts,
for love was also my loss,
my muse was just there to use,
and leave an empty light,
but my soul did put up a fight,
and these nights alone,
I light a white candle,
so I can remember,
not all of us get forever.

Talking to God

Lights cast holy shadows,
shimmering over floorboards,

God speaking softly,
casting an immortal glow,

for suffering is beautiful,
ebbing into a torrent bow,

bending but never letting go,
these nights alone in the desert are beautiful.

Atlas a Mind Opens

She betrayed our eight years of love,
Smiling and kissing a fake face,
lust drove her desire,
pure animal instinct,
sex for hire,
I worked my fingers till they bled,
and never fed my desire,
After heartache and three days of sorrow,
I am set free with the power of positivity,
take my love for granted but you can't take my glow,
for even the angels are jealous of my bow,
I cast many men underfoot, ate the bullet,
and pushed on with my life,
lonely doesn't describe the joy,
the birds sing now,
and the stars they align,
For you thought I'd take my light?
Glock loaded and locked,
yet family is my life,
I will show a stubborn world,
what love, true love, can do,
because we all hurt,
and love can take the rue.

<u>As the Sky Hides</u>

The sun didn't come out today,
forgotten in gray,
too dull to play,
walking on a sea of thoughts,
I am home, yet lost,
stones, catching my thoughts,
when I am alone,
a drink in hand,
I am trying to formulate the master plan,
some people wonder if I am truly Superman,
can we all fly away?
To sunshine and rainbows in a hollow sky,
forget the gray, the rain,
make peace with the hate,
take a day, to formulate the rage, caged away,
articulate the stage, light the path, and walk away,
for a broken man is a better man,
sometimes we need pain to understand,
that everything is OK and we can always heal again,
we can always feel again.

Sowing a Field for Harvest

Seek thy gate,
for the host is removed from place,
cast thy glare and remove thy fate,
For energy cast your hate,
unwinding in the master's way,
That we should forget night and seek day,
For our life force does not stay,
we bleed our will day to day,
and maleficence is the savors way,
You sow a crop that will not stay,
for hate is hate,
and love is way,
And ignorance is the only true mistake,
for life we live,
and life we take,
but each new day,
is the one we make.

Codded Gods

I write the faith my soul has cast aside,
for mortal sins are a lie,
God is not part of this world,
I hate the Christian faith,
I hate the Christians,
and I prosecute them,
I hate humanity on an abnormal level,
I am your God yet you refuse to believe,
For I am made of everything,
you rebuke, you bow, and grovel,
Yet I have judged every molecule you have walked on,
I have observed your DNA, your being, and changed code,
I am the God you do not know,
For I speak,
and all of this programmed world changes.

Wheel of Dharma

You let the dark in,
now it silently consumes,
My inspiration is my curse,
for death will touch down,
softly kissing my face,
I will be laid down,
ever so softly, as Gaelic drums beat,
Upon a gallant ship will I go,
flowing over the torrent of humanity,
to be brought back,
pulled back into the flow of energy,
and put in a new body,
soft, warm,
small, fragile feet,
with no memory of my past,
to haunt my fresh start.

War in the States

God has become politics,
lost souls, dead children,
searching for material wealth,
caring not for our nation's health,
All I hear is left this, right that,
Hatred is how we act,
We need a true leader who will bring back,
humanity from the dead zone,
Racial hatred is prosecution,
We, you, and I,
were all born free,
Humankind added the shackles,
My sins are not my fathers',
Your sins are not your fathers',
We breed inequality and fly a high flag,
Honor was a warriors mentality,
He fought,
he died for you and me,
yet I don't see us free,
Unite a nation under blood,
we are all but one,
a drop and indescribable speck,
for we all deserve respect,
and many nations want to bring us to our knees.

Advice to My Younger Self

Don't give up on your dreams kid,
yeah, moments aren't always bright,
life happens and people die,
people hurt you, abuse you,
you fall, you get cut and bleed,
but you got to keep getting back up,
work your fingers till they bleed kid,
hold on to that dream,
sometimes you can't eat kid,
earn it, work for it, and make mistakes,
rewrite the moments you dream of,
because you are great kid,
truly great,
and moments can blind a great man,
making him give up and become lost,
hold your dreams,
and kiss your lover,
it will all work itself out you'll see.

<u>Yearning in Stillness</u>

Secret songs of distant gods,
haunt a being alone in an empty void,
for he is chained from wrist to feet,
shackled with unbreakable iron,
awaiting a god's return who never showed,
he stands alone in silence,
until every angel can hear his soul,
his power rivals the gods who chained him there,
yet a tear falls as he recalls
the last immortal song
whispered to his soul as a goodnight lullaby.

<u>Old Roads</u>

Thoughts bleed poetic blood,
so much in life is misunderstood,
for life it plays like Hollywood,
on an unending loop of lies,
For true love still has its lullabies,
pacifying a being to stillness,
replaying the very first kiss,
when the wind fluttered by,
For all men see are dollar signs,
selling old faith at the crossroads,
It leaves a vast vase empty,
until the wind chips away its mortality.

Mad Hatter

Can barely stand,
broken from the master plan,
of everything I am,
I am not through,
in the sense I seek you,
looking back from the stage,
Gunshots scatter the,
last who matter,
Lives dissolves as,
the Mad hatter takes the stage,
waves of broken laughter,
roses scattered on the stage floor,
Bullet shell casing found by the back door,
as the night hazmat crew mops up bloody floors,
the news comes on and gives a story,
about a man stricken with grief,
who knew they could never leave,
with the closing curtain,
He was certain,
He gunned em all down.

Serpent's Sky

Dragon fire claimed the skies,
igniting fear and casting pyres,

For we awoke,
on a smoldering stone mound,

Elegant gold with scales to the ground,
rage has cast his crown,

Filled with rubies and emeralds around,
he hoards his wealth from human sound,

All who tread here are never found,
for fangs consume and flames abound,

In primordial rage he set the immortal stage,
for a champion to cast him down.

Memory of Eden

How does one tread into Eden,
knowing the path is lost?
For knowledge was gained at life force cost,
And the winds sweep the garden's trees with eyes of frost,
In the plentiful bounty of heaven's boss,
Eve had killed the moment's thought,
stealing her desire to be like God,
Was it right from wrong,
that cast the spots?
Was temptation even wrought?
For the earth sings in many clocks,
and brings death from many cloths,
Do Angels still guard the sacred stop?
For we are locked out of heaven's lot.

As Hell Calls

Static crackles against the night steam,
For Satan searches his next to screen,
Torrents of abominations crawl,
And all who search see their fall,
A clawed hand finds its way down,
over the mouth, silencing sound,
Cold as death's touch bound,
lost in sleep not yet found,
For abomination's teeth bite the proud,
Bleeding neck to vileness hound,
and pull free under the siege of dreams,
For valentine's day lovers find their feed,
and hell is let loose,
as Satanists bleed.

Damned by Fire

Golden stairwells march up strewn glow,
for mortals walk the path below,
and heaven's sky is all for show,
for he walked the path with God,
studying his mortal rod,
Angelic light had cast his bow,
and in the dark he hid his soul,
for wings were given and minds were sown,
For he hated anything that was whole,
and it was God he struck,
that broke his trust,
and cast out he had become,
But he remembered,
the hand he raised to strike his face,
was the charred hand,
used to wipe his race,
and in the dark he held embrace,
with broken wings he killed his faith.

Broken Harp

For halo's eternal glow,
killed the sun and brought the snow,
dooming man down here,
to put on a show,
Each new dawn has brought the ghosts,
that watch our race down below,
For we evoke fire's passion,
And we freeze in hallowed silence,
shivering in an essence wrought by violence,
Peace keeps a true man's heart,
so that when we restart,
All is not lost in whole.

Current Dominion

For power haunts a lost man

ebbing into a dream

to wake a life and never sleep

to feel alive and never weep

to whisper to sweet cold damned nights

to finally free one's mind

in memories we are called upon

in moments we are strangers

to welcome eternal sleep

we keep our minds in square hallways

hoping to find the way out

we are alive but doubt

the existence of God

we are taught a nameless world

we bring a nameless curse

because our time runs out

we are victims of repetitive abuse

because we design our world

we furrow our brow

and cast the now

and never walk

in the current of power.

<u>Forgotten</u>

I ebb into dimly lit walkways
holding my lover's hand
time has forgotten us
we share a bag of popcorn
lights dim
holding hands
as the reels click on
no one but us, alone
people walk by and gossip
cold winter air outside
the feeling that everything is a dream
awake yet fighting sleep
hard times befall me
as I seek work
thinking of her
my own life, Maria
I am the slum boy
singing in her ear
begging her to never leave
but we part before the sun kisses the blue sky
I wander alone in my mind
pondering the meaning of beauty
I search for so many hidden truths
just to fight the Christian world
she is part of God
his servant
and I am nothing but void
pledging my existence to the old gods.

<u>A'an light from a Rose</u>

Ebbing into your power
your soul haunts the depths of my eyes
casting a glow to shower
even a blind man
I search in empty, dark moments
to hold your outline
for you paint my muse and evening sky
you damn my thoughts and leave me
shy
searching for the words of your beauty
has left me with a journey
passing through eternity and time
I search for God and I am left to find
we embrace the dark but search for the light
you calling my fading name
and I am left to blame
for every night devours
the last of all our powers
and your being has brought
the last to bloom
the eternal flaming flower.

Last Who Fell

Cast from grace
falling through purple lightning
to watch the robes of God descend
waking up mortal
in a land of immortal suffering
to know such strife and never-ending life
to watch as love is lost to life
we bring our death in gray skies
we seal our fate with our lies
and cast our stone with last goodbyes
to call his name in vacant cries
for hell, it walks, and Satan tries
to keep your flesh
your sin his pride.

Society's Illusion

Sorrow sweeps an empty face

for men beg to leave this place

loss and poverty leave its wake

as life haunts and takes

in snow and morn we adorn

the last who call from hollow's wake

chaos haunts the moment in which we dwell

for our waking moments we breathe in hell

monsters we ensue onto the superficial

for we chase the image of the artificial

we seek capital gain

to change a system designed to take

we gossip and talk and breed our hate

to cast many a life and doom its fate

we bend a knee and preach a need

to find he has no faith in us

we search awake but never dream

to sink our minds in the webs we weave.

<u>Seek in You</u>

For energy has but one need

a vessel to feel free

a way to bend minds

for lost souls try

on the path to enlightenment

to atone for sin, grief, and sorrow

for we wake up but never see tomorrow

we are blind to the path of light

for our universe it dwells in night

it breaks the stardust to torrent way

for God, he exists but has forsaken stay

to walk amongst us and give us way

we forget our minds

as bodies break

seek in you for you are sought

to master life

and heaven's plot.

Pandora's Mist

Walking alongside the cosmos
to behold the stardust in infinite view
for we seek dreams in which
water falls off the side of the universe
trees of life dwell in mist-shaped forests
for worlds are for exploring
fire dances in the velvet sky
as glow bugs churn and say good night
the mist shrouds the secret light
for paths we walk to sacred heights
in shooting stars we dream of a view
in fleeting skies we hum a tune
we are one with it all
to pull in hallowed bright
and cast off the dark in every night
for secrets keep our hallowed might
and power shimmers in every lost child.

<u>Flute of Anubis</u>

In the desert sands the gods dance

and sweep the wind

while holding hands

they wake the Jinn and make their plans

as spirits walk the empty lands

as breath is brought to hallows wake

Anubis speaks through sacred break

in sand and dust the giants wake

to make the dunes

the human's grave

in all his ways Anubis calls

in sacred voice from mountain halls

he wakes the dead for as hens they sleep

to follow him as deserts weep

he plays his flute in one last tune

to call the sky

the sun

and moon.

Disk of Aten

For his river in the sky it watered the earth and all the rye

he drank the sun in the falcon's cry

For god he walked as night time lied

illuminating the rays of life

he struck the moon

his sacred wife

to shine his shadow of hallowed might

he drank the prayers of all who fell

for god he walked in sacred shell

in shadows he would reflect the light

to guide the souls

home at night

he brought gold to the desert lands

and taught the people to use their hands

engraved on mankind's throne was his name

in solid gold

Aten the god of all that is shown.

Duality of Truth

Wisped onto the cosmos
torrents of fading matter
paint my world of blue
for I am a liar
to convince myself I am true

In vacant doorways, I am brought
in shadowy steps, I am thought
dissolving in everything I've sought

We bring a world through hallowed might
to draw a muse
and lose a fight

Battling the monsters of reality
to seek an answer that is duality
searching a void for peace
we leave a rose at the feet
of a fleeting universe.

<u>Halls of Knowledge</u>

waking moments torment a sacred dream

from which we choose to forever sleep

awoken a man finds worlds

brought unto his doorstep

truth lingers in his mind

should they exist

he shall find

he has to rewrite the beginning of time

knowledge is paradise and prison

keeping a man's world in check

for when reality knocks

at the gates to enlightenment

will he run?

Or will he enter?

Race of Jinn

Smokeless fire cast

a mold from sand and glass

a world adjoined but apart

to create a world of Jinn

they came too and naught

flash binding and hot

to smother the world of man

they fathered children with man

and cast magic from their hands

erasing memories of long ago

for temples had they built

and men had they killed

to remain a lost secret race

for every hallowed moon

they pass the veil and move through

the mirror in every room

look away child

for if you stare

they will stare back.

<u>New Day</u>

Echoes of voices lost
call back to follow us
the grand design of human trust
amongst jungles where serpents lie
to see a world through a broken sky
for we bring our day
and forget our night
to bring a world where creatures fly
we sing our ancestral song
to remember where we belong
we try for peace but forfeit the strong
willed child
we fade in havoc and forget to smile
for we are sunshine in cloudy skies
we are dark in the morning light
we are coffee-stained pages
that shout our resolve
we are peace problems solved
for light fights back a damned world
and free-spirited beings twirled
the cosmos unrelenting
to create a song
for us to dance and sing along
forget the hate
make peace stay
and make sunlight shine upon each
new day.

Warrior's Will

Keep your chin up kid,
some nights you have to go to bed hungry,
just remember you are great,
keep working your fingers to the bone,
you have the making of greatness kid,
hold onto your dream,
when love abandons you,
know, trust, you will find a different world,
awaiting when you wake,
you won't always wait in the cold,
shivering, cold hands, cold feet,
breath the only warmth,
sitting in a cold car praying you could,
know kid, you are the shit soldiers are made of,
tough, solid, metallic,
your will, wrought iron,
I will instill kid,
a morbid sense of reality,
you're not a superhero,
you bleed, you break, you mold,
you lose, you love, then grow old,
you take nothing kid,
but try for it anyway,
it's the journey that counts,
don't wait your whole life trying to be somebody,
become,
when your warrior awakens it shall be.

<u>Hold On</u>

Hey you...
standing there in the clouds
so afraid to be found
looking so lost
life's dragging you down

Hold on...
to moments you know
if only you could hold me
you'd know...
it's the memories we carry
too afraid to
let go...
life isn't scary

Let's go...
let's fly away to a better day
where we own the moment
where sunshine
finally stays
and every ray is a bead of light
and every memory we
finally, make it right
Hold on...
don't give up on the fight
love feels so right
as you're holding me so tight
So hold on...

Hey, you...
standing there in the clouds
you're free
finally, you found me.

<u>Damaged</u>

So close to the top
starving in tundra snow
holding a candle of desire
not to be the best
or even great
not to watch the world be so fake
I wasn't set to sing you lies
I wasn't brought to torch your skies
I was simply put
and here I am
standing beneath a starlit sky
watching dreams play out
watching people get found
watching so many beautiful things
none of which I am
I sing a broken man's melody
pain has forged me
resolve has stayed my hand
and rope has set my fate
to die by who I am
I am solidified
in your daydream
maybe when we wake
I'll be found.

<u>Starlit sky</u>

I froze for your
heart's earnest blue
watching every moon
to sing heaven's tune
tundra hue
and damned be the bluest eyes
set to watch you.

Burning Nights

I can feel your mind
imprisoned in mine
holding hands through time
we find our love
part of the grand design
we create our paradise
we rewrite the book of life
take our hearts and play
the soldier's wife
we take our lives
to brand new heights
and remember the lonely nights
where we walked through hell
cigarette burning
yearning to be together
how we're learning
the hell
that our families made us walk
but they couldn't stop
love.

Racing thoughts

Dreams of long ago
won't let me stop
ebbing in power flow
haunting my past
to hope I can last
in a race of shows
to dream a dream and bring you eternal glow
to chase your mind with
the spirits below
to find you with me through time
to watch the beauty of everything redesigned
to make amends with love's plans
to find out who I am
the money didn't buy me peace
the money just brought more greed
why can't you see 9-5 you're not free
but chains hold a rich man
in the aftermath of who I am
I am standing
afraid to wake
for dreams do take
the soul with every
bone to let us know
we're here for sins we cannot
atone.

You can have the world

You can have this ball of light
spinning ever so bright
so many times you were right
I picked a fight with you
but all I ever wanted was you
all I ever sought was you
my Madonna glowing in a hallowed tree
How free she was in everything
I seek her peace so many
paths
she was there just to let me know
it will never last
and at last
she saw past
the artificial glass
broken on the floor
slamming every door
searching for my poor
ass holding her so tightly
every night
and praying
to never let go.

Chilled Vindication

You tore my world apart
you broke my fragile heart
slaying a monster you created
to protect you
you tore my mind not seeing
I bled and starved for you
I was not free
wearing your shackles
because of love
you whipped my back
as I was bent over on my knees dying
I called out in rage
sitting broken
freezing to death
not cold
my sin on my breath
realizing all love will leave
death does not describe it
you were alive
and you died
I was there
I saw you cheat
I didn't understand
why you broke our plans
I didn't understand why you made me stare at my gun every
night
but I understood that God
was right
I was leaving.

Waves of Siren's Way

Gold of lost ages
sat beneath the frothy sea
to wander with fortune and
hold the last key
Olbita sanctioned in love
to mourn its gold lost to the cove
for legends tell of sirens' way
who drew the maps to find the gaze
sunlit hue hell's ablaze
of a blue diamond to be amazed
it sat for 300 years churning
rolling on the seaweed bed
the pharaoh's ship
the crew all dead.

Grains of sand

Has pain yet becometh?
To drain thee by sorrow
Has the rain not ceased breath?
To bring thee another tomorrow?
Has thy destiny threaded
into the depths that are hollow?
As thou wander barren
has thou forsaken grace?
For it was I who made
thy day.

Honor in Faith

Hallelujah's sacred chant
of angelic love
echoes on
the broken man on one knee
he lost his wife, his job, and his health
yet he fought against ill will
he fought to bend his broken knee
the pain it brought him was hell
yet fractured and tormented
he was free
he sang the words in every key
Hallelujah...
Hallelujah...
I am going home.

Desert Road Home

Rending the blood-soaked pages
on the face of many stages
I feel the gifted being misplaced
with no way home
many nights on a desert road
wandering lost sweet soul
driving through the rain
wishing fame hadn't
called their name
chilled moments hold them
to know them
would be to
walk alone
under the starlit sky.

Rendered

Damned be our moments
haunting the essence of God
we once felt
cold dark hallowed night cast
a memory of a man
we become
then we leave

for wakes shake
the moment
pain casts the bottle
rage casts the man
and sin casts the mold

we speak our truth to atheistic worlds
where the spirit does not exist
in the cold empty
void we are told we go

your sky, your stars, and even you
are oceanic movements of shadows
for materialism drives society
lust, drugs, sex, and money
are the four gods you hold

the flame of another life dwindles and is snuffed
with regret for not having followed
Anything of value
for atheism cannot give you purpose, and God
cannot give you emptiness.

Valor

Choose your God choose your smile
broken on earth for a while
remember the days of sunshine
where loved ones' memories hold you
remembering their breathing
walking down memory lane
their hands raised to you
now they're gone
but they guide you no less
building R.C. cars with Dad
reminiscing a life well lived
and every favorite song
a family man through and through
who believed in the power of the sun and the moon
oh man and the food
the long cookouts with family still smiling
he was a great man
and it is God who now holds his hand
granddad now and immortalized in ink
but damn he made us think
what a blessing to be part of his family.

<u>Illusion of Freedom</u>

The dawn of man
has no such plan
for arrogance repeats
a life cycle
faithless men breed war
science has conquered mankind
to fuel the killing machines
seek not the world
for it will betray you
power-hungry countries
no better than tyrant kings
seek to control
to suit their desires
life has no meaning
as eternal darkness sweeps through
a haunting melody echoes on the wind
illuminating the dark
"Tread softly my child"
it sings
poverty was designed by men
we have enough to feed a dying world
we refuse the light
and live in the era other bastards have designed
people have made up your worth
but you are priceless
control was built as a system
to oppress
as we are given illusions of freedom.

King of Thunder

Shango thunder's king
calling the sky blue
painted it with lightning
as a powerful amulet consumes
the family of his lover
grief had guarded his heart
walking in
the great sea.

Her Breath on My Skin

How do we survive the pain
when our hearts are ripped out?
Vacant places of frozen hell replace our emotions
when love dies, when the angels who carried our fate
surrender to death
How do we breathe suffocating on the smoke of our lives?
How do we embrace ourselves walking alone
under the torrent of a howling moon
to walk alone breath showing in the chilled air
love abandons leaving a fucking shell
leaving a walking hell
her memory etched on my breath holding her so fucking tight
every day was all right 'cause she was right there
now gone
torn from my essence numb hallowed fucking demon
chasing the ways of angry men
cutting the pain with liquor
smashing bottles in rage
staring at a moon that can't hear me
screaming in my head
my dreams are fucking dead
and in the wake
I follow.

Runic Hammer of Fate

The rubble piled high
so close to the sky
The artifact they sought
was a flat golden hammer
Turning runic light to words
In hand it gleamed golden brown
for light cast off it did not make a sound
Voltan reflected off the broken cloud
An utterance cast the bound
sending him to Hades
Standing over broken corpses
He was raising them from eternal sleep
Chaos his friend would often weep
for life had its secrets
and this wouldn't keep.

Flesh of Immortality

Am I your savior or damnation?
For all flesh goes to me
whether or not you believe
every comic order ordains
all the chaos of pain
Loss is etched on your face
for bitter hearts cast the blame
be it love or loss it's all the same
not one thing you control
through misty shells of all I know
foreshadows a place far from here
for every thought it is so clear
tasting upon every tear
not one yearns to live
and lose its fear
for life is not
but death is near
so seek a way
that's not from here.

Old Glory

Every thought echoes upon the mist

walking through the cosmos

wrath has quelled the simple man

holding the broken plan

of where fate meets

for most of us are never free

we speak our fate to time

we bind our minds with rhyme

to break a place we shouldn't be

we see our hearts and how they bleed

fate leads us away

for bitter men had wished to stay

in the current of now

fading old men

telling of how

their predisposed vision ran the world.

Rose We Leave

Follow me child of the universe
wishing for a dream
for we are lost in the deepest sleep
we cannot know a future of suffering
for we wish the pain away
but here we stand in the broken way
here we stand in the falling rain
here we stand with all our pain
for we lose the ones we love
we grow old and suffer
we stare at blank walls and walk
in the memories of our past.

<u>Fires of Truth</u>

Place dead roses on my grave
in the cave where I lie
for truth is an ugly monster
hell is this place I wake up to
hell is the monster within that consumes
greedy people stealing the future
hell is life
for its fire refines
but makes you not want to live
waking up with no purpose but to exist
is as good as being dead
for in the wake of our lives
we take silence with us.

Fleeting Life Force

we search for life
rejecting the concept of God
for we fail to recognize the building blocks
we do not give life as we think
for all is gone before we blink
we will run from a dying planet
to a home among the stars
to float in deep space
the last of a desperate civilization
running for their lives
peace is not in the cards
for we rebuke the light
the light that brought life
the light that brought death
we welcome a home in a sky that will not abide forever
we fail to welcome true life
for we are weak
we think what we are told is true
to push the boundaries
but are deceived
for no life can come from death
that which we are
once we have broken the shell
only then will our hell
subside.

Beautiful Monster <3

Sitting in an empty lawn chair
soaked in alcohol
your thoughts haunt my god damn fucking mind
drinking to numb the breakup
eight years running through my mind
god damn the black hair falling on my face
you smiling
the sex we had for hours till the sun rose
family who said they would never betray but did
floating drunk with pistil strapped
knowing my life is ending
driving 122 on the highway to forget
now living a life of poverty
working my ass off because your father instilled a work ethic
in me
hating him because I am not free
I tried to die but my atheist listened to God
living with family
going through jobs like water
met a new woman
begging me to love her
but I can't
because I don't want to love anymore
still we're set to be married
and I want her to know
I am broken because you didn't have to kill me
you destroyed every aspect of me instead
I am alive but dead
I tried to love but failed

I am what you say
a beautiful monster.

91

Passage of Dead Roses

love that shakes an empty space
filling voids in all its places
to know love and sweet embrace
to stay with her through all the stakes
for time it takes
and love it breaks
to find true love
in all it shapes

we search for heaven
always pretending
to never have enough
but cold and naked we walk
down a path of dead roses
to deliver the truth

under the sheets we tell
our secrets
for love is an imperfect monster
dealing all the cards
and life it breaks

Death it takes
to make a life well lived
want to leave this place.

Lost Type 1

Humankind has evolved to find
history repeats
from nowhere we have come out of
evolution a guessing game of sorts
for maybe we were type one
through time
but the savage nature of human will
has killed many a world for greed
and thrill
if we fell to planets through
which we escaped
to find that time has just erased
our footprint on the cosmos
or we were brought from stars far away
to be imprisoned with no escape
condemned to think we walk alone
our DNA structured to let us know
we were created.

<u>Axe Tribes</u>

The smoke fills a war-torn sky
tribes gather
then collide
war eats into the Viking blade
for Valhalla's queen shall have her way
for mead and axes
cut a path
and warrior's way
shall forever last
in the valley of Odin
for the prophet's song
trance unto seer's ways
chosen
have frozen the last of
the berserker race
for braided beard
and tattooed face
have left the world
without a trace.

5150 Misanthropy

I dive in a way
wishing my body won't stay
I fucking hate the Earth
cancer grows
coughing blood on soaked pages
smiling knowing
I am dying
because I hate people and the world
I made a difference they tell themselves
but the exit's the same
knowing the rainy summer days
when I walked in silence
peace comes
As I lift the pistol
and take it all away.

<u>Moments in Time</u>

I miss the energy in your thunder
Laden skies adorn
the king and kinsman
who wear the thorns
Lightning flashing a purple hue
for rain it chants
the Templar tune
and in misty trails
of mountain paths
I see the sun
written
on your staff.

<u>You Broke Us</u>

Everything you say
makes me want to stay
but I see
no need
with liar
hands
that way

wish every night I was OK
broken from the tragedy
your memory
haunts me

save my mind
but I find
reason to rewind
our past in place
but I can't escape
your face
the way
you move through that place

broken reasons still haunt my hands
broken pieces of who I am
I see the hands of every man
that touched our love

so broken

all the memories of us
fell to the floor

can't ignore
the warning lights
even though it felt so right

every hallowed moon felt so light
every single June felt so tight

you broke my mind
you left the world behind
the two of us
spinning ever so near

faithful is what you're not
that much is clear
it took everything I had to keep you near

now you're gone
as I try to move on
I am stuck in your
Love
I am stuck in our wake
I am stuck in this place

I am stuck in our
earthquake
breathe in
its all
rain
smiles fade
as I erase
our memories.

Her Shadows on Empty Walls

Save me I am calling
through hell falling
like the last heart beat
you say you don't need
me
it's true you're better off
in so many ways
wishing I could erase
the late nights we must
face alone
no turning back
can't replace us
watch as we fall through dying skies
tears fall
hurt her and made her cry
buried my pain inside
sealed my alibis
watched the last good nights
alone walking through snow
god damn
I am alone
so many times I tried to let her go
memory still on my mind
can't let her know
I think about us in my free time
Everything we had was fading
hearts turned to black
no staying
in place with no love
just saying
it was the two of us
now it's gone
strap your boots on and move on
soldier's song

in love with the war
love is pain but it's all
for
the one we name
casting blame
and hate
onto a blank page
in our minds
trying to be alright
trying to be sober
on a damned night
calling out
your name
follow
me
god damn
this place without you
is all the same

I can't erase the broken glass
I can't erase the past
I can only drink a glass
and cheer you
from afar

fading lonely star
trying to stay with you but so apart
wearing love like a scar
emptying emotion into the dark
maybe one day
we'll get a fresh start
leave it all and let it fall apart
but for right now I just shiver
your mind shot me with every arrow from your quiver
it's dead love we deliver.

Alone Along the Coast

Late nights
catch me
playing pretend
better off dead
searching
for the last of my medicine
trying to be well
thoughts driving me mad
knowing I am going to hell
pages left empty in the book
where I am left speechless
no less
god wishing you well
god damn too much pain to
even wanna feel
get behind the steering wheel
drive to the empty sunrise
thoughts playing through my mind
don't know what's real
don't know how to deal
every single night a blur
the last of the alcohol calls
as I fall in mountain halls
sinking in your memory
caught on repeat
this isn't me
different light
different life
why can't I see?

Isle of Ink

Because you blossom you constrain
for even the wind will push the rain
ensuing the thought of bloodthirsty stain
constricting the conscious flow
to delirium the vibrant show
for delectable the fierce sun glows
and even the ferocious rose
shall wither in broken prose
to coarse with bewitched crows
flying in the empty snow
for energy gathers and then lets go
leaving us to slant our nose
for only God knows
the broken way
our life grows.

Way of the World

I cannot search for you
for you are not here
in a way dormant to oblivion
sleeping on the changing winds
you have made me strong
honest and hardworking
yet I hate and respect you
thoughts are lost to time
time is every man's god
for it dwindles and is snuffed out
yet I serve despair
for one can only withstand so much torture
I batter my broken body against the stones
hoping to get up
to have one more chance as the waters try to drown me
exhaustion, pain, strength,
it creates beautiful suffering
so beautiful and yet so broken
like a moon cut in half
and a light slowing going out
the beauty will be imprinted in my mind
and when it is my time
I shall scatter my broken being
amongst a warm starlit sky.

A Dream Upon Time

For it was my home
often dreamed when alone
to walk along the road unknown
where reason finds time who owns
the stars, the sky, and all the gold
for we wade in shallows fearing the depths
for most of our lives we dismiss our deaths
we drink our peace in all its ways
we torment our minds another day
we bend our peace and reap the hay
to feed the life of all our hate
to speak a name in all its way
escapes our mouths and falls astray
for we are
but not enough.

<u>Wadding in Midnight Streetlights</u>

Remembering the nights I spent alone
walking under a moon rounding
the city glare sounding
so mixed a tone
A note I left
to remind me of all I know
So lost
yet
so found
Broken down on a foggy night
love beating in my chest
felt so right
So long
have I been gone
to mix hope with a forgotten love song
to know
a beating heart glow
surrounding me
to finally escape my mind
and then find peace.

A Fading Dream of Her Love

Hallowed light of a thousand roses

weep at your going

for you were the moon

that no longer shines

you were the stars in all their glory

you were the life of the universe

now we wade in empty expanse in your wake

for life gives but then it takes

leaving a broken man

missing you in a haunting aura

for she will be remembered

long after I fade

penned in ink

for the old gods to find.

Buried Secrets

Call to me shadowed child of the abyss

for I drink your tears

I hear your prayers

many a god was created

but men chose

the ones that suited them

we exist in a shadowed path dormant

waiting for a lost soul to open the gates

for

blessing await

while we erode in time.

Free Will

Song and rhyme often find the patterns of old minds
humming their peace in the void
for the world has forgotten the light of Old
gods
paving a path for self-righteous hatred
breeding in gatherings
old men damning the world
who have no real power
they cower and bow to the crown
never seeking a free mind
they seek a hive
with one leader
listen to the wind gently rustling the night leaves
feel the sunshine on your face
and set a path for truth
be it mine or yours
seek your gods
for we dwell in the abyss.

Old Gods

For old gods waded in caverns deep
lost to time and laid to sleep
covered in stone monuments
the last to walk the green pastures
is now long gone
for no one would truly recognize a god
In society it is the unattainable
the figment of wild imaginations
for fire catches myth
and drives the inspiration
the belief that we will go on
even when the gods
are lost to time.